FRISCO
the
THREE-PAWED PUP
FINDS HIS FRIENDBEASTS

Frisco the Three-Pawed Pup wakes up and thinks,

"TODAY IS GOING TO BE THE BEST TODAY EVER!"

Frisco thinks that every morning, actually,
and if you ask him, he's always right!

But this morning, Frisco knows he's really, really, REALLY right. He just KNOWS that today is the day he is going to find his **Forever Friendbeasts**.

Forever friendbeasts: [fur-**EV**-er frend beests] animals that walk on 2 legs and give dogs

Frisco has lived at the shelter for more months than he can count on his one front paw. He wants a real home with his very own Forever Friendbeasts more than anything.

... love and treats and food and scratches and treats and walks and treats and treats ...

The first possible Forever Friendbeasts to come
into the shelter stop right outside Frisco's door!

Frisco jumps up

and spins in place,

which is always a Friendbeast favorite.

The family smiles and tells Frisco what a handsome and strong pup he is and how well he's doing. But they, like so many other possible Forever Friendbeasts, walk past him to meet the other pups... The four-pawed pups.

Frisco flops back down.

Another possible Forever Friendbeast enters the shelter, but this time, Frisco's room door opens. This Friendbeast actually wants to meet Frisco! Frisco's puppy heart dances with joy!

Frisco charges out of the room,

but as soon he does,
his front paw slips out
from under him and

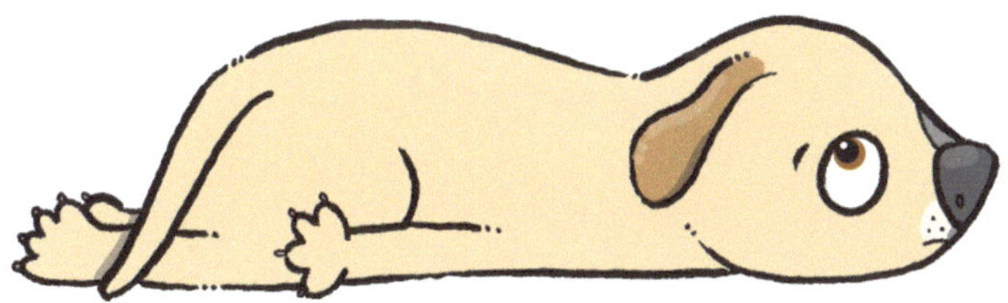

Frisco falls to the floor with a thud.

The possible Forever Friendbeast quickly becomes "the human formerly known as the possible Forever Friendbeast" as he walks away explaining that he needs a dog that can keep up with him.

Frisco wants the chance to show how much he and his three paws can do!

But the possible Forever Friendbeast is already gone.

Frisco decides he is going to be a perfect pup when the next possible Forever Friendbeasts come in. The problem is that Frisco doesn't really know what a 'perfect pup' looks like!

He tries sitting up straight.

He tries bowing.

He tries smiling.

What the heck is 'perfect' anyway?

Then Frisco sees a little leg next to him. The leg of a Little Friendbeast! And Little Friendbeasts usually come with full-sized Friendbeasts.

There they are!
The Friendbeasts have dirt on their legs!
They must have been hiking! Frisco loves hiking!

The Little Friendbeast scratches behind Frisco's ears.
Frisco loves scratches behind his ears!

But most of all, Frisco LOVES Little Friendbeasts!

Frisco is so excited he forgets all about trying to be a perfect pup.

He jumps up on the
Little Friendbeast!

That wasn't good,
but what's worse?
His front paw slips out
from under him when
he lands and he falls!

THAT wasn't good,
but what's even worse?
When he falls, he falls right
into a full-sized Friendbeast,
knocking her down!

Frisco squeezes his eyes shut for what feels like a million minutes.
He knows the possible Forever Friendbeasts are already walking away.

But then a little hand pets his head and a full-sized Friendbeast says,

These Friendbeasts don't see Frisco as a dog with a *missing* paw.

They see him as a funny dog with a huge heart that will be the perfect addition to their family.

They can't wait for the adventures they will have with him and the three paws he *does* have!

It happened! It really happened!
Frisco has finally found his very own Forever Friendbeasts!

And everything was perfect.

Frisco is happy from his nose to his toes
and as he falls asleep, he thinks "I was right...

"TODAY WAS THE BEST TODAY EVER!"

I AM FRISCO
THE THREE-PAWED PUP
AND I'M THE PUP WHO
NEVER GIVES UP!
I'M DIFFERENT, IT'S TRUE
NOT WORSE, NOT BETTER
AND I KNOW THAT TODAY
IS THE BEST TODAY EVER!

FRISCO
BEST TODAY EVER

MEET MY FRIENDBEAST
(also known as the author)

My Friendbeast's name is Katy. We live in Utah with another full-sized Friendbeast, the Littlest Friendbeast, and a drawer full of puppy treats!

Katy wrote this book because she hopes more Friendbeasts can be like **ME**, focusing on the paws they **HAVE** - not the paws they don't. She also hopes I can inspire Friendbeasts to see each other in the same PAWS-itive way. And I hope she gives me more treats!

She is very good at playing rope tug, finding good off-leash trails, avoiding rumble strips while driving, and finding the tastiest treats!

Katy made a website so you can learn more about **ME** and find more fun **Frisco the Three-Pawed Pup** activities and books!

FRISCO'S FOTOS

I LOVE sticks!

I LOVE pizza!

I LOVE The Littlest Friendbeast so much!

Keep up, guys!

Me being SO CUTE!

My happy place!

NAIL TRIMS!
*ANTS!
RUMBLE STRIPS!
HEAT
BEING ☆ UNDERESTIMATED
SWIMMING
(SPLASHING IS WHERE THE MAGIC HAPPENS)
THE DOORBELL
MED
LOW
STOKE

TAKING BATHS
UM
HIGH
METER
TREATS!
HIKING / BEING OUTDOORS
NAPS!!
THE LITTLEST FRIENDBEAST
EAR SCRATCHES AND BELLY RUBS
TREATS !!!
JUMPING UP TO GREET NEW FRIENDBEASTS
SNUGGLING WITH FRIENDBEASTS ON THE COUCH
AND TREATS!

Every book in the Frisco series is dedicated to Frisco himself,
who every day reminds me – and each and every Friendbeast he has ever met
to focus on the paws that we **HAVE** and not the paws we are missing.

First Edition

Hardcover: 979-8-9897118-1-9 | Paperback: 979-8-9897118-0-2

Published by **Three-Legged Dog Life**

Illustrations and design by Missi Jay, Gigglebox.net